# The Flowers of *Gratitude*

## Love and Gratitude of Guruji Maharaj

Kamlesh Aunty ji

Published by

**Hawk Press**
4836/24, Ansari Road, Daryaganj
New Delhi – 110 002
Phones: +91-11-23278618, +91-11-43667199
E-mail: thehawkpress@gmail.com
www.thehawkpress.com

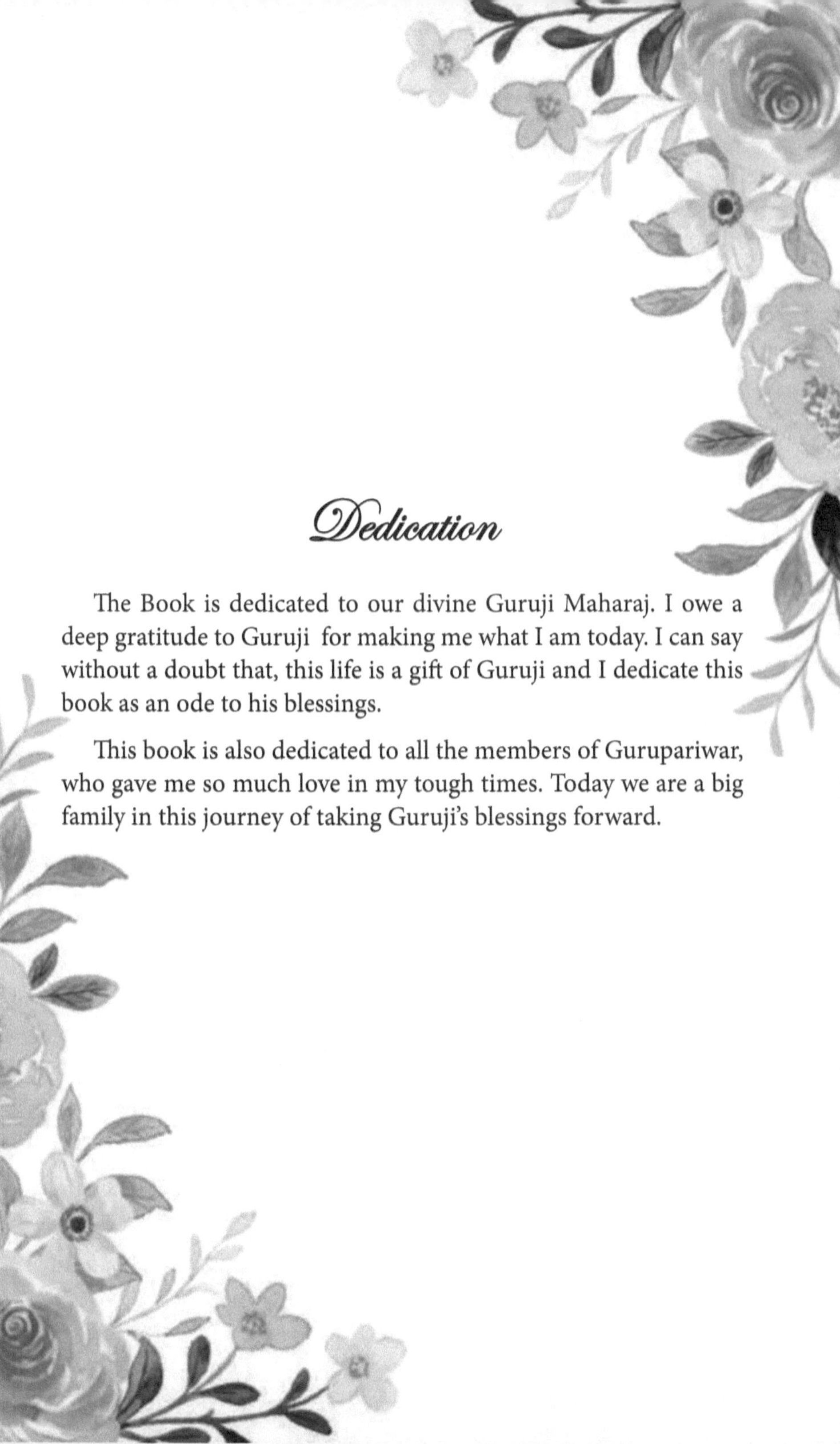

# Dedication

The Book is dedicated to our divine Guruji Maharaj. I owe a deep gratitude to Guruji for making me what I am today. I can say without a doubt that, this life is a gift of Guruji and I dedicate this book as an ode to his blessings.

This book is also dedicated to all the members of Gurupariwar, who gave me so much love in my tough times. Today we are a big family in this journey of taking Guruji's blessings forward.

# Contents

# About Guruji Maharaj

गुरूर्ब्रह्मा गुरूर्विष्णु: गुरूर्देवो महेश्वर:

गुरू: साक्षात् परं ब्रह्म तस्मै श्री गुरवे नम:

The Hindu Shastras say that to attain Nirvana, a Guru's handholding can create life. This journey of life is now a dedication to my beloved Guruji Maharaj. In the vast ocean of the karmic world, I, too, am showered with immense blessings in life so much that I feel confident and full of gratitude to put these thoughts into ink. For me, Guruji is more of an emotion, a way of life that transformed my thoughts, beliefs and karmas today to lead a life of joy, fulfillment and gratitude.

As we call him Guruji Maharaj, the Mahashiva was a Shiva reincarnate in human avatar as Nirmal Singhji Maharaj. He descended on earth to help millions of mortal devotees to shower his blessings on July 7, 1952, in a small village Dugri in Sangrur district of Punjab.

As a famous saying in North India- Poot ke paanv paalne main hi dikh jate hain (The kid's traits can be identified right from his cradle)- Guruji Maharaj, too, showed his godly traits of divinity right from his childhood.

Guruji's life and his story need no formal introduction, and the very fact that one more literature is being presented to the world on his life, this time with my hands, by His grace, is proof of his godly stature. I still would try to verse my little knowledge about him. Our Guruji Maharaj's stories of healings and miracles are not just known to my countrymen in India but also been a talk of the world since the time he came to the aid of millions of his followers to help them lead a blessed life.

Jai Guru Ji

Yet, if I try to touch this widely known topic from the surface level, then Guruji's earlier life was all about spirituality right from his childhood, and his godly aura could be seen by the people around him.

Right from childhood, Guruji Maharaj found joy in the company of saadhu sants of his village, which often worried his parents. Like normal parents, their concerns were genuine about his education, and worldly duties. After completing his education as per his parents wishes, Guruji renowned this materialistic world. He followed his soul's journey to help the lesser mortals like us to sail through the vicious cycle of life and death- Nirvana and worldly duties.

Guruji, with his medium of prayers and meditation, carried multiple miracles in his lifetime. Nothing was impossible for Guruji, and he showed the way to righteousness and faith to supreme to his beloved devotees via Satsangs, Sangat and Seva.

In his small lifetime, he visited various parts of the country to heal and bless the devotees. The major place where his footstep fell most often was Chhatarpur, and later on, he made his temple in Chhatarpur, Delhi, also called the  Bada Mandir. Guruji established the Shiva temple here and also took his Samadhi here. Guruji Máharaj took his Mahasamadhi on 31st May 2007 in the same place. Though he left for heavenly abode, his disciples still feel his vibrations and presence when visiting the Bada Mandir.

Without spending much time in his introduction, which is widely available on multiple platforms, I would like to express more of my personal experiences that led to huge transformations in my life due to his Sangats and Satsangs for a long time devotee.

People around him have witnessed his miraculous powers in daily lives as he was growing up. The stories of his godly powers transcended the borders of Punjab soon and traversed through the entire globe. The stories of his appearance and disappearance are normal tales among those who have been fortunate enough to see and know him in this mortal world. He could know the person in and out just by looking at his aura and bestowed upon his blessings as he thought fit for him or her. Even without touching a devotee, he could bless them by transforming their life's path; his blessings have been benevolent enough to cure and heal his devotees without asking them. Such was the love and dedication of our Guruji Maharaj in the life of his devotees!

He soon began his Satsangs and daily Sangats. His blessings travelled not to just whom he knew but to those related to him, even after he has shifted his abode to the other world today. He is a kalyankarta whose energies and vibrations have been elevating and miraculous to even those who can think of him. Millions flocked to him for treating their diseases, misfortunes, financial and emotional problems.

As one of the supreme power and Shiva reincarnate- Guruji, descended on the earth with a mission of relieving all of us from the never-ending cycle of life and birth via our clean Karma's. His belief in cleanliness was not just limited to the surroundings, but he believed in it in letter and spirit. The cleanliness of the core- the soul, the Karma is of utmost importance to help in attaining Nirvana.

Our Guruji Maharaj guided a way to many in attaining this salvation by working on our humanly cardinal vices of Kaam, Krodh, Lobh, Moh and Ahankar (lust, anger, greed, attachment and ego).

My connection to Guruji Maharaj has been eternally transforming and full of gratitude. This connection is now a soul connection that has brought me to this stage that I wish to pen down my thoughts to recite to the whole world how our Guruji Maharaj can be a torchbearer to others lives.

More and more ascetics like me can transform their lives by his blesings and lead a life of more joy, fulfillment, and peace. So, this book would be more about those godly experiences and teachings of our beloved Guruji Maharaj to spread his teachings to a maximum number of people in this cosmos.

That would be one of my Seva as a token of all his blessings in my life!

प्रेरकरू सूचकश्चव वाचको दर्शकस्तथा।
शिक्षको बौधक षडेते गुरूव: स्मृता:

प्रेरणा देने वाले सूचना देने वाले सच बताने वाले रास्ता दिखाने वाले
शिक्षा देने वाले और बोध कराने वाले ये सब गुरू समान हैं

# Prayer

"Prayers are the very highest energy of which the mind is capable."

— *Samuel Taylor*

The world knows the power of prayer. We have heard the stories of manifestations of our thoughts into miracles due to our prayers. So, do you pray? What exactly is prayer? Here is my interpretation of prayer that I have understood from my 75 years of life. As I wrote previously that I spent a significant time of my life in the seva of Guruji, my meanings of prayers have also been much more simplified now.

Prayer doesn't just happen when we kneel down or put our hands together and focus only on what we expect from God. As per me, thinking positive and wishing good for others is a prayer. When you hug a friend, that's a prayer. When we send our good wishes to our near and dear ones and say that drive safely, that's a prayer. When you help someone in need by giving and energy, then we are in prayer. When you forgive someone by your heart, then you are praying.

So, for me, prayer is-

- Prayer is a vibration
- Prayer is a feeling
- Prayer is a thought
- Prayer is a voice, a Love.
- Prayer is a friendship

- Prayer is a genuine relationship

- Prayer is an expression of a silent being.

This is what is my version of Prayer!

"Every positive thought is a silent prayer that will change your life."

— *Bryant McGill*

# Guruji The Creator

"When facing the toughest battles, toughen up and trust God, the Almighty."

Often, we do not understand the meanings of the events in our life, especially the bad events and our trust in the creator; the almighty falls short, and we start doubting our faith. This is one of the mistakes we do in the process of spirituality.

We do not understand that everything that happens in our life happens for a purpose, and there is definitely a reason hidden behind it.

I have learned in the process that we need to trust Guruji's plan. Our beloved divine Guruji Maharaj is the creator of the universe. He is Mahashiva- the best planner!

We need to be grateful to Guruji for both the good and the bad times. He knows the best reason behind these times. If you trust his ways and believe in him, you will always be thankful to Guruji Maharaj, just like me.

With each struggle and hardship, Guruji will make you stronger and wiser. Today we might not see it with immediate effect, but there will come a time when his perspective will make much more sense to us.

Sometimes the events in our life may be happening to give us the lessons of our life or sometimes to make us stronger for the upcoming time, or sometimes it may happen that our experiences will be useful for someone else's growth in the future. We might not know the exact reason, but that doesn't mean that reasons do not prevail.

With my experience, I can vouch that Guruji decides only the best for us. Trust his process, plans and ways, leave it on him and forget the rest. Surrender to His Will!

The creator knows the best-Guruji Maharaj!

"The hands that made the stars are holding your heart!".

# My Journey with My Divine Guru Dev ji Maharaj

"How I Met My Beloved Guruji Maharaj ?
The Spiritual master is the mercy representative of the Lord."

— *Srimad Bhagavatam*

As everyone has problems in life, so did I have. One day I mentioned my problems to one of my friends, who was my neighbor. She suggested that don't worry; there is a Guruji in Jalandhar who solves everyone's problems.

So, I decided that I will go and see him and find the solution to my problems. My friend's maternal home was in Jalandhar; so it was easy for us to put up in Jalandhar.

The day came when I had to meet my destined Guruji Maharaj. It was a Sunday. We reached there at 10 am. In the vicinity, soft Shivji's Bhajans were playing. Shivji's pictures and a statue were beautifully lit, and it was a very pious environment. The vibes were very different, and the environment had wishes and blessings spread all around.

All of a sudden, whisperings began around me that "Guruji has come."

I looked around to see where Guruji was. I couldn't see the Guruji anywhere. To my surprise, a young boy in his early thirties came and sat on a wooden chair. He was our Guruji!

I couldn't believe that such a young boy could be the Guruji. Since I couldn't believe it, so I again asked my friend if he is the Guru. She stopped me from asking this question as everyone was looking at us.

He was a handsome, fair and tall man in a brown safari suit. His aura was very attractive; one could be glued to him. I looked at him with my eyes wide open, thinking and looking at him in awe. At that very moment, I could feel that yes, He is my Guru. I was sure that I have finally found a Guru.

As I was thinking this, a voice said

"Kamlesh tu ki sochni hai ?

Main Guru lab laya?

Nahi. Tu nahi main Guru lab laya."

You must understand that you don't find a Guru. He finds you. He makes a connection. We do not have the Aukat to do that. This was how I got connected to my Guruji in year 1984. The old saying proved to be right that day when I found my Guruji Maharaj.

"When the student is ready; the Guru appears."

# My Journey with the Divine Guruji to Kailash Mountain

Now, I want to tell you a very beautiful incident of how I travelled to Kailash Mountain with my Divine Guruji, and I could envision the real roop of my Guruji in a moment of devotion!

Going to Guruji's Ashram in Jalandhar was very tough in those days. I used to stay in Arjun Vihar- an Army colony- Dhaula Kuan. To go to Jalandhar, we used to walk from Arjun Vihar upto Dhaula Kuan, take a bus to ISBT, then to Jalandhar. The state bus service was really poor in those days- no doors and window panes were broken. Due to this, we bore the hot air-loo in summers and cold air in winters, and it troubled us a lot. Local people traveled with blankets and quilt.

But I was determined to visit Guruji despite these hurdles. I never cared for these hurdles on my way. Guruji gave us the strength to reach him, due to which it was fun to bear those difficulties. Youth, too, gave the strength to reach the divine Guruji.

We used to reach Guruji's Ashram in the afternoon. The Satsang used to get over by then. Guruji served Langar to those who came from outstation. Matthi from Lovely Sweets was always served as our Guruji was also very fond of them in the food. Malpua was his favorite sweet.

It was late in the afternoon; Guruji asked me if I went to see the Dasvaan Dwar. I didn't know what daswaan dwar was?

One day, I told Guruji that I want to know about him. Guruji smiled! All of a sudden, my eyes were closed, and I didn't know where I was. I saw that I was walking along a path on which I saw a beautiful garden, full of flowers, beautiful fountains and surroundings that I never saw in my life. The beauty of that surrounding couldn't be expressed in black and white.

After crossing these gardens, I was on the gravel ground when I lifted my eyes. I saw a huge mountain as I started climbing. Suddenly, I saw a mountain covered with snow. I kept climbing the mountain higher and higher. As I climbed more, I saw something eternally mesmerizing

I saw the half-moon, and also I saw Shivji, who turned to Guruji.

I could see them simultaneously- Shivji and Guruji! As I was climbing higher and higher, there was only white light all around me. Suddenly, my regular clothes vanished and were replaced by a long cloth wrapped all around me. Then my eyes opened!

When my eyes opened, I was in Satsang, and Guruji was sitting in front of me, and I touched his feet. He said-

"Kar aaya sach khan de saar"

"Oh!jada kapda badla san thanu moksha deeta"

# New Sangat

"When you put God in charge of your life, no one can take you out of line."

My uncle was posted outside India-Canada. I used to join him there often.

This time when I came back to Empire Estate, there were lots of changes. New Sangat had joined as Guruji always mentioned to get a new Sangat.

When I reached Empire Estate, I saw a young boy near Guruji. I asked someone who is he? I was told that he is some fauji. I saw that Guruji was looking at him with all the love in his eyes. I could feel that his heart was full of love for him. Every gesture of Guruji was oozing love for the fauji.

Guruji took out one garland for him and put it on the neck of that young boy. Seeing all this love, I was very jealous for a fraction of a second, but then I realized soon that, like all of us, he is getting his share of love from Guruji. On my further inquiry and curiosity about the special treatment to him, I found out that he hails from the Navy and his name is CDR. Sharma.

After some time, I shifted from Delhi to Gurgaon. I received a call one day.

The voice said- "Is it Kamlesh Aunty?"

I said- "Yes, I am Kamlesh Aunty speaking. May I know who you are?"

The call disconnected.

It happened again. The phone rang.

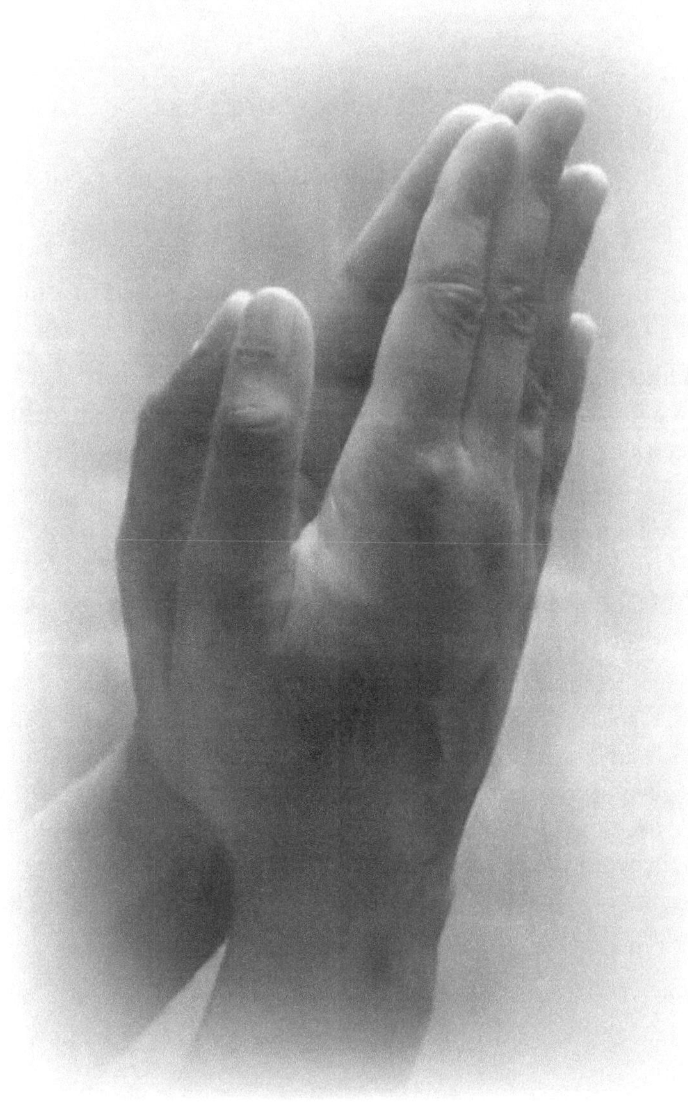

"Is this Kamlesh Aunty?"

I said- "Yes. May I know who you are?" I again asked

Unfortunately, the call again got disconnected.

The telephone rang for the third time, but this time I recognized the voice and

I asked

"Who are you looking for?"

I am looking for my Kamlesh aunty', He said.

"You will find her, but first speak to me and tell me who are you?" I told him.

"I am CDR Sharma speaking," He said.

As I told you that he knows the best and has the best plans for you, this too had a reason. This was how I was introduced to Gurgaon Sangat by CDR Sharma. Truly! Guruji always chooses a person and opens the path for you.

# Mishri Prasad

"The value of consistent prayer is not that He will hear us but that we will hear Him."

— *William McGill*

Some anecdotes remain in our memories forever, and they remind us of the greatness of that moment and the value of someone in life. One such incident in my devotion was the Mishri Prasad incident that remained etched in my mind forever.

It was a very old Satsang in Empire estate in Jalandhar.In the Satsang, one uncle and Aunty visited Guruji very occasionally- CDR Banerji Aunty and Uncle. The couple had no child and were worried due to this.

One day Aunty asked Uncle to request Guruji for the blessing of a child. As per Aunty's insistence, Uncle requested Guruji to bless them with a child. Guruji replied- "I will bless you with a child- a son, but remember one thing when he will turn 21 years old, he will try to kill his father. What do you want, a son or a husband?"

Guruji waved his hand in the air, and suddenly, his hand was full of Mishri Prasad.

Guruji handed the Prasad to Aunty and said- "Take it as Sachidanand ka prasad".

Aunty extended her hand forward and took the Prasad. Her hands were full of prasad, and some of it fell on the ground. Seeing that the Prasad was falling on the ground, she took the prasad in her saree and started picking up the rest of it from the floor. Guruji said- "What is in your hands is yours, and the rest of it is for the Sangat." This was how we received the Mishri Prasad for the first time from divine Guruji as his blessings!

किमत्र बहुनोक्तेन शास्त्रकोटि शतेन च ।

दुर्लभा चित्त विश्रान्ति: विना गुरूकृपां परम् ॥

(What is in saying a lot? What is in crores of Shastras?

Without a Guru, gettting the peace of heart is impossible)

# Guruji Permission is a Word of Almighty

"Blessed is the One Who Trusts in the Guru, whose Confidence is in Him."

Some incidents make you believe that great people are not just recognized by human soul but also from the nature around us. They bloom in a way that their fragrance lightens up the entire humanity. Guruji was one such soul.

Guruji had a friend who was a Brigadier in Army. He was posted in Jalandhar. He stayed in  Army quarters in the cantonment area. The houses were pretty old, made from Britisher's time. They looked like barracks. The drainage system was also not very robust, and the water from the open drainage used to get collected in the gutter.

Guruji often used to go and stay with Brigadier Uncle. Guruji took a bath near that open drainage. The water always overflowed from the drainage. Over time it happened that a plant grew near that open cemented drainage. The plant bloomed beautifully and kept growing with lots of leaves and fragrances strangely.

Very soon, uncle got retired from Army, and he had to shift to his own house in Chandigarh. As a symbol of Guruji's grace, Brigadier Uncle took the plant with him and replanted it in his Chandigarh home.

"Blessed are those who have the gift of a Guru- one of God's best gifts".

# This Moment

"The only way to survive eternity is to be able to appreciate each moment."

*— Lauren Kat*

Your only reality is This Moment, Right Now and Right Here! The secret to health for the young body and soul is not to mourn the past, not to worry about the future but to live in the present moment mindfully and purposefully.

True wealth is the ability to experience the present moment fully. No other time and place are real. You can find lifelong peace and abundance in such simple awareness.

There is profound wisdom to this. There is a reason why all the enlightened souls, right from the Buddha to many other mindfulness meditation teachers, have focussed on the present moment. Yoga is one of the techniques meant to bring back to the present moment.

Buddha defined enlightenment as freedom from suffering. He understood very early on that that most of our suffering is created in the mind. We create our suffering ourselves with how we think and deal with the present moment.

Hard times come to all of us, but we can choose how we respond to them. Just because you justify your sadness/ anxiety doesn't mean you have to take the bait. You can choose a different response in Now.

You can always choose to smile and laugh through the hard times. When there is pain, you can deal with it right now.

Dive into it and feel it and express it so that your next now is not painful. Cultivate the best now.

"Forever is composed of Nows."

# How Guruji Maharaj Removes Our Past Life Debts

"Nothing happens by chance; everything is pre-programmed, in order, in accordance with the law of nature."

We all have karmic debts and we need to clear them in the present life to move to another level of spirituality. Unless and until those karmic debts are paid, your growth is standstill. In one such incident, I could understand the real meaning of karmic debts and how a Guru can help you to clear them by propelling you on a certain path.

It was an anecdote long back when we were sitting in the company of our divine Guruji Maharaj. One of his devotees Gandhi Uncle came to meet Guruji Maharaj to complain that he is suffering from stomach pain from a long time. Guruji Maharaj listened to his problem patiently and told him to come back after some time.

After two days, he returned again with the same complaint and Guruji Maharaj again said the same thing that come after some time.

Every time he came, Guruji Maharaj kept giving him another appointment for six long months and this way almost half a year passed and he kept getting the next appointment.

One day he again came and he said something to Guruji Maharaj. On listening to that, Guruji Maharaj poked his fingers in his stomach and his pain vanished forever.

Seeing this magic, he said to Guruji- "if you had to poke fingers in my stomach, then why did not you do it six months before? I had to suffer so much and also spend 70000 Rupees to doctor."

Guruji Maharaj explained to him —"In the previous birth, you had taken a debt of 30000 and 35000 Rupees from a doctor who cured you. You didn't pay your debt to the doctor. That's how you paid 70000 rupees to him. Once that doctor's debt would be over, you will be alright."

I got to know this story when I went to Dubai for a Satsang. I met Gandhi uncle there and he mentioned the same story that how he came to Dubai to see the doctor.

After listening to the story, Gandhi Uncle went to a Satsang and headed for the Langar Prasad.

Now his visits to the doctor have lessened and he is much better now!

This is how a Guru can sail you through your past karmic debts and take away your pains forever.

"Good actions, good results, and bad actions, bad results. What we have received to date and currently receiving, all are only the fruits of our actions."

# Guruji Saves You from the Crisis

"Do your best. Then, surrender to the Divine Will."

This is one incident that reinforced my faith and belief in Guruji that he can sense the dangers in your life and would stand in its way to save you. He becomes a shield to protect you. This incident happened like this-

As I was a regular visitor to Guruji's Sangat and I never missed an opportunity to visit whenever I could. This time also when my uncle boarded the flight to Canada. I had a longing to visit Guruji, and I went to Jalandhar straight after the flight to be with divine Guruji.

With my medical reports, I went to Guruji. The moment I saw Guruji, I caught his legs and feet and cried my heart out.

"Guruji, my children are small. They need me," I said

Guruji said-"Don't worry. Nothing would happen."

Guruji, I have heart disease, and my one pulmonary and one ventricle is half blocked."

I stayed there for some time. Now it was time to go. I took Guruji's permission to leave. Strangely, Guruji told me to wait and leave after half an hour. I couldn't understand, but still, I waited for half an hour. After an hour, I took permission and left for my home.

As we reached Karnal, we saw a huge bus accident there. A bus had toppled upside down. To my surprise, it was the same bus I had decided to board a few hours ago that Guruji didn't allow.

My life was saved by Guruji that day! It was Guruji who delayed my plan for an hour to save my life.

So, if you surrender to Guruji, he will take care of you and save you from any unwanted incidents in life. Have faith in your Guru.

"A man must have faith in the Guru's words. He succeeds in spiritual life by looking on his guru as God Himself."

# Karmic Retribution

"I Bow at His Feet and Constantly Pray to Him, the Guru, the True Guru has Shown me the Way."

This incident is about a big lesson that I learnt from our divine Guruji Maharaj and want to share with my readers. I will tell you one such incident where I was convinced that Guruji's blessings can sail a person from past, present and future karmas.

The incident proved to me that it is only Guruji who can free you from the sins of your karmas, whether they are this birth, past birth or future births karma of even 100 years. So, we must take his blessings to seek redemption and atonement.

One day, an Aunty had her Langar and one small boy was sitting opposite to her. This boy was eating less and spilling more. Aunty watched this small child that he was not eating properly, so she felt pity for the small child. After finishing her Langar and keeping her plate back, she decided to help the child in feeding him properly.

She kept trying her best to feed him, but he kept on doing the same thing -eating less and spilling more. So, in the end, she stopped trying and went to keep his plate back.

The Sevadars watched her closely and as she stood up to keep his plate back, one of the Sevadar stopped her and said- "Aunty, this is your child, so you will have to consume the remaining Langar. We don't encourage wastage at Langar".She was quite disappointed in hearing this and tried to convince the Sevadar that it was not her child and she was just helping him finish the Langar. However, despite her earnest efforts, the boy didn't finish his food and kept spilling the food.

Clearly the Sevadars were not convinced. So they forced her to eat the remaining food on the plate. Aunty was in a crying situation, but she somehow ate the remaining jhootha food of that boy.

After she finished the boy's Langar, she obviously marched to Guruji Maharaj and cried her heart out to what happened just before. Guruji listened to all her story and nodded his head and said, "I cleared your next birth karmas; otherwise, you would have been born as a pig in your next birth!"

Aunty was clearly very surprised to hear this. Guruji further explained what happened and it was amazing to hear!

He said that —"It was not the four Sevadars who forced you to eat the langar, but there were five of them and I was the fifth one— the child! So the child was me who was helping you get clear of your karmas.

Guruji further said- "Main Tera Agala Janam Kat Ditta; otherwise you would have been born as a pig. I only made you eat my jhootha food".

This was the power of Guruji, who could alter a person's present, past and future karmas. So, have faith in Guruji's divine ways and keep doing your karmas. Guruji is with us and he will do wonders in your life.

"Realize That Everything Connects to Everything Else."

— *Leonardo Da Vinci*

# Guruji Gives You at a Proper Time

"You never know where a blessing can come from."

When you ask something to God or your Guruji, it may happen that you may not get it at that time; rather, it comes to you when the time is right. So, one must not be disheartened. You must have faith in Him that only the best would come to you at the right time.

I will tell you one incident where the ways of blessings and the timing of blessings became clear to me. I learned that Guruji Maharaj often gives you what is best for you. He gives you much more beyond your expectations.

Guruji Maharaj is much far-sighted than what we can even think of. We often ask for only worldly gains, but sometimes he offers us what we can never think of in our imagination.

One day I went to Guruji Maharaj with a box of sweets on my uncle's promotion. My uncle has become a Squadron leader.

Guruji Maharaj already knew everything about the promotion as usual but he still asked me who is a Squadron leader? I explained to him the Army terminology as he was much familiar with it.

I told Guruji Maharaj that he had become a Major equivalent in Army. After that, he will be Lieutenant Colonel, Colonel, Brigadier, Lieutenant General and then General. He asked me a strange question whose answer gave me a lot of clarity regarding my various spiritual development questions.

"Okay! So can't he directly become General?", He asked with a child-like curiosity.

I said -"No Guruji. We reached that height only with experience. This year's long in gathering knowledge will make us reach that height of career", I said

He further explained to me the logic of things in a very interesting manner.

"If you will give the MBA books to a child, he will not understand it. He will have to reach that level to understand the MBA Knowledge. In the same way, as you join Guruji Maharaj for the first time, you are in his KG class. He takes our exams and makes us pass from one level to another level."

"Reflect upon your present blessings — of which every man has many — not on your past misfortunes, of which all men have some."

*— Charles Dicken*

# Blessings can do Wonders

"When prayers go up, blessings come down."

Our divine Guruji's life was all about blessing the mortal souls like us; People visited him from far and away to get free from their old diseases or solve their problems. It was normal for us to see and hear such miracles. One such miracle we saw in front of our eyes was about a man who used a wheelchair and visited Guruji.

One afternoon, we were all sitting with our divine Guruji in the Empire estate and were listening to his Satsang. One uncle came to visit Guruji. He used a wheelchair. As Guruji saw him, he said

"Aa Gaya?"

He bowed his head as he saw Guruji. Guruji too blessed him

Guruji asked- "kee galva"

He said- "All your blessings Guruji."

Since it was a Langar time; So Guruji gave him the Langar Prasad.

He said- "Guruji, I can't eat this as I can only eat very light food like Khichdi or Daliya".

Guruji told him- "Take just one bite," and he ate the full Langar to his surprise!

As Guruji got up, the man said -"Guruji, I am in a wheelchair for years."

Guruji stood up. He pulled him from the wheelchair and made him stand and walk for few steps.

To our surprise, he started walking!

All this was real and was happening in front of our eyes. I think we were too blessed to be a part of this process. This was the last time the man used a wheelchair and he began eating normal food after this incident! Do you know who he was? He was the owner of Apollo Tyres! This was his level of blessings of our divine Guruji.

The Mahashiva roop could do anything.

"Worshipping the feet of the Guru is the ultimate of all worships."

# Satsang Miracles

"No one, even he might be as great as Brahmaa, Vishnu or Shiva can swim across the ocean of existence without the guidance of the Guru."

— *Goswami Tulsidas*

Guruji's miracles had trespassed the local boundaries, and people from far lands came with their ailments and diseases for the cure. Like Shiva, who drank the poison for the betterment of humanity, Guruji too took people's problems on him and blessed them with health, happiness and prosperity. His methods of treating an ailment were very different. Guruji used to take everything on him and always blessed his Sangat. He took the sickness of Sangat on him, whether it was somebody's stomach ache or any other illness.

In one such incident, one day, a couple came to see Guruji in Sangat- Aunty and Uncle.

Aunty was ailing from skin cancer, and she had turned all black. Guruji looked at her and made her sit in front of him. After that, what we saw was no less than a miracle, and that moment is still vivid in front of my eyes. As Aunty was sitting in front of him, Guruji started turning black, and Aunty's color turned white! Guruji turned so black that he took all her cancer on him.

After this, Guruji went away suddenly and came back after one hour. We were very worried, but he was alright when he came back, and only a small patch was now left on left side of his forehead. Even today, we can still see it as one of the visible signs on his Swaroop. Do you know who that couple was?

Aunty and uncle were the owners of Mahathta Hospitals!

I recited this event to you to narrate one of such incidents of Guruji's benevolence and blessings on his devotees. The list of his miracles and blessings is so long that we can only count the blessings of divine Guru Ji Maharaj today !

"Without The Blessings And Compassion Of A True Guru, The Path Of Liberation Is A Distant Dream."

# Beautiful Blessings Always - Mama Ji

"Difficult it is to ascend oneself into the state of the Supreme,
without the compassionate blessings of a true Guru!"

— *Varaha Upanishad*

I would like to tell you about a very sweet incident where we saw the Mamaji roop of our divine Guruji and how it was personally very touching. This anecdote remains very special to me.

Once I was in Jalandhar for Guruji's darshan. Sangat was coming and going. I sat for the entire day as I was an outsider. For such outstation Sangat, Langar was served in the day and chai Prasad was served in the night. Guruji used to say in his famous words- "Peele Prasad hai"

We saw that one family has come to see Guruji. The family had four members-Uncle, Aunty, two boys having the age 8 and 10 years. Guru ji got up himself to receive the family. Uncle touched Guruji's feet and the children embraced Guruji, calling him Mamaji. Guruji put his arms around aunty as his affection.

The family was welcomed very warmly and Chai was offered. We got to know that Uncle's name was Darshan Singh from Patiala.

It was amusing to see the children sitting on Guruji's chair on his lap and shoulders while addressing him as Mamaji. They were with us for one hour and then they left. Guruji went to see them off in a white Maruti. After seeing them off, we saw that Guruji had been standing at the gate for quite some time.

When Guruji came inside, I asked Guruji the reason for standing so long at the gate. I was very touched to know the reason. Guruji said that he was blessing labor working outside. He was not well. He had to work so that he can buy food for his family at home. If he is sick, then he will not be able to work. So, I needed to bless him. I was highly touched by this gesture.

After that Guruji came and sat on the chair, Chai was served, and he restored his energy. I asked Guruji about the Mamaji relation with those children, and during that conversation! I revealed one of my wishes to Guruji.

I said-"Guruji when I am born again, I want to share a mother with you. I want to share the same mother as you have!"

To my surprise, Guruji smiled and looked at me. He was having tea at this moment of conversation, and I cannot forget his smile. He was smiling from his eyes full of compassion. On this gesture, Guruji gave me his tea and said—"Le Chai Pee Le, Aj Ta Tu Meri Bahan!"

This was the most special Chai I had in my life and the first and the last time I shared the same chai with Guruji. I was so blessed with that Chai.

Darshan uncle is no more now. He called me Gudiya, which means my child. His boys have grown up now- Rajendra and Raju! They live in Patiala now.

In Patiala, Guruji's Darbar is downstairs on the first floor. There is one bedroom and a washroom. We hear some unusual things from Sangat about it.

One of the things that people tell is that when you are sitting on the ground floor, even today, you can hear the sound of water splashing as if someone is having a bath. Not only that, every day, the towel is moist, and the soap has froth. The bed sheet is found crumbled as if someone has slept on it!

Such is the beautiful blessings that Guruji has left for us even after he has left his abode.

"When one finds the true Guru, one can conquer half the world."

# Guruji's Ways of Healing

"Although the world is full of suffering, it is also full of the overcoming of it."

— *Helen keller*

Guruji was a healer. His mere putting his hands on someone's head could heal a person to the core. His healing tales had travelled far, and people from all over came to get themselves healed from various ailments. This tale is also about one such healing incident we witnessed. His ways of healings were unique.

Meeting the divine Guruji Maharaj was like spiritual energy entering our soul. It was the soul food. To enter the Guruji Maharaj Darbar in Jalandhar was a soul-cleaning experience. It was the medicine to the ailing soul. Just the act of sitting there looked like all the past life Karma was getting washed away by the blessings of divine Guru Ji Maharaj. We spent a mesmerizing time in Guruji's Darbar.

Guruji had unique ways of healing people you must have never heard or seen before.

To heal, he used to take a spoon in one hand and a fork in another hand. He always took the fork in his left hand and the spoon in the right hand. Then he used to bang the fork and spoon with each other and saying "Aaja!" After this, he used to take them to his room.

In Guruji's room- he had a bed and a takshaposh with whose help he used to cure people.

Guruji made them lick the takshaposh and then moved the spoon on the Vertebral column.

We got heat and beautiful vibrations from the spoon, which he moved on the spinal cord. With the movement of that spoon on the back, the disease used to vanish. I can tell you this with my own experience that cannot be expressed in words.

Guruji used to wear a big Mala. Guruji used to dip the Mala in the big steel glasses with the humming Sound of Guruji. After that, each one of us was offered the glass of water in which he made the Amrit Prasad. This glass used to have a very different fragrance in it. This was the way the Sangat used to get the Amrit Prasad.

One such day an uncle came to Guruji Maharaj and said- "Guruji, my son  drinks a lot of liquor. Please help"

Guruji put the Mala in a glass of water and offered it to his boy. The boy straightaway refused to drink the water. Guruji insisted many times that he should at least smell it. The boy accepted, and he smelled it. Then he looks at Guruji and gulped it immediately in one sip, and the problem was solved.

"Kayoo tainu apni whiskey da swad aaya we"

These were unique and magical ways of healing Guruji Maharaj used to treat People. He could see these wonders in a moment, and these wonders had the potential to change anyone's life in just seconds.

"Every step taken in mindfulness brings us one step closer to healing ourselves and the planet."

# A Blessing of Self Contentment

"Be Thankful For What You Have; You'll End Up Having More If You Concentrate On What You Don't Have, You Will Never, Ever Have Enough."

A human being is an entity whose urges for worldly life can never get over, and he is never satisfied. His desires and wishes keep on growing in life, and there is no end to these desires. Guruji taught us the concept of Self Contentment- an important lesson for happiness and ending miseries in life. I would narrate one such incident where Guruji put an end to my limitless wants and desires and gave me the blessings of self-contentment.

One afternoon, we were in Sangat with Guruji in Jalandhar. Langar was served to all the outstation people. I had many things on my wish list, and I wanted Guruji to bless me with all the wishes. After the Sangat had left, I took the opportunity to ask for my wishes to Guruji. I was adamant about the demands from Guruji. I was under the impression that I am of the same age group, and it would be easy for me to demand from Guruji.

I was completely wrong in my notion, and it was not an easy task. Guruji said that after so much insisting, let the right time arrive, and you will fulfill your wishes. I could not understand its meaning.

Guruji got up and started to walk. I was still adamant about my demands. I held Guru Ji's legs as he was walking. I kept on dragging myself by his legs to not let him go until he blesses me with my wishlist.

Suddenly, he stopped. He said —"Okay. Leave me now". He kept his hand on my head.

That moment was life-changing for me. I can't express the self contentment felt at that moment and after that gesture forever. This was the last time I asked Guruji of something. There was no asking after that, and I received everything on my own.

Such was the blessing of Self Contentment by our divine Guruji Maharaj! Lots of Love and Blessings.

"The greatest wealth is to live content with little."

— *Plato*

# How Guru Ji Killed Your Ego

"Dissolve your ego before it dissolves your self"

Ego can hamper your Guru Bhakti. When you surrender yourself to your Guru, you should also surrender all the dark parts of your personality to your Guru like ego, guilt, anger or hurt. They can come in the way of the end goal of Guru Bhakti. I will narrate an incident where you will realize how a Guru doesn't differentiate between his Bhakts and he only wants you to surrender to him with faith completely to him.

An Uncle used to visit Guruji Maharaj. One day he also brought his cousin with him

As his cousin entered the Darbar of Guruji Maharaj, he bowed to him from outside the door and entered the Darbar. Guruji Maharaj welcomed him with lots of affection as he always did with any other new Sangat.

This cousin performed Guruji Seva in such a passionate way that he became his favourite very soon.

The cousin was always very happy with the thought that Guruji Maharaj gave him so much seva, but strangely his Uncle had started becoming jealous of this fact very soon. He observed how the cousin is doing seva wholeheartedly and how Guruji was giving him more and more seva.

This thought started entering his mind that he has been coming to Guruji Maharaj for so long and Guruji Maharaj has given all the Seva to his cousin and not him. He was always murmuring it to himself and cribbed a lot about it.

As Guruji is Antaryami and he knows everyone's mind, one day Guru ji called him and made him sit in front of him.

He said- "Come and give all your ego and jealousness of your heart to me."

Guruji Maharaj further told him that- "You know one thing that the moment your cousin entered the doorstep he simply surrendered himself to me and uttered in his heart- "You are everything to me from today. You are my father and I have come under your shelter. It is only you who will do everything for me"

This is called total surrender to a Guru, which is why he is my favorite disciple. You are yet to surrender to me in the same way as your cousin.

Then Guruji Maharaj blessed him with lots of love and affection. Guruji Maharaj killed his ego this way!

So, we understood how Guruji could make you polished like a gem of a person. We learned that when we enter a place of worship like Gurudwara, one must be humble and leave everything to the wish Malik or AImighty. He will take care of you.

"We come nearest to the great when we are great in humility."

— *Rabindranath Tagore*

# How People Treat You is Their Karma and How You React is Your Karma

"Keep Your Face to the Sunshine and You Cannot See a Shadow."

*— Helen Keller*

We all come across some nasty people in our life and sometimes they can really get on our nerves to make the situations really complicated. We get confused in that state as to how to handle such kind of people. Here is my take on handling such energies-

When people get nasty with you, it's usually best to walk away from them. When someone treats you in a dirty way, do not pay attention to it and do not take it personally. I will tell you why-

There is a famous saying that nothing about you what lot about themselves. This saying clearly conveys that how the other person behaves is not about you but them.

No matter what such people do or say to you, never drop down to their level.

Rather than the mudslinging, you must know that you are much better than them and just walk away from them. People will treat you the way you will let them treat you. You cannot control them, but you can definitely control how much you can tolerate them. You must control what you tolerate.

Beautiful things happen when you distance yourself from negative people. Doing so does not mean that you hate them. It simply means that you respect yourself.

One of the most difficult tasks in life is removing someone from your heart but remember that a relationship is a waste of time. The wrong people teach you the lessons that prepare you for the right ones.

So, just a kind reminder to you that no matter what such negative people do to you or say about you, you must keep shining as you always.

"Negativity is an addiction to the bleak shadow that lingers around every human form--you can transfigure negativity by turning it toward the light of your soul."

*— John  O' Donohue*

# The Mahashiva – Guruji Maharaj

"Nothing is everything, and everything is nothing."

We call our divine Guruji Maharaj as Mahashiva- the reincarnation of Shiva. Like many devotees, I, too, was grateful and blessed to see and feel the aura of his Shiva reincarnation. This was the day I felt immensely grateful to Guruji to make me see the real Guruji Swaroop- The Mahashiva roop. The incident goes like this-

In those days, GURUJI used to stay in GK 2. From time to time, Guruji used to isolate himself for ten days to heal himself.

To heal people from all over, he used to take the Sangat's diseases on him. He used to clean himself from all these diseases which he took on him in those ten days. It was his cleaning period, and no one was allowed to enter the Mandir. As I was unaware of it, I went to the Mandir on one such usual day. A young boy looked after the Mandir in those days.

He told me-"Mandir is closed, and GURUJI doesn't meet anyone."Since I had come from very far, I said- "I will rest for a while and will go back." He agreed. As I was resting, I fell asleep.

All of a sudden, I felt a bright light in the room. I saw that the Mandir was in the basement, and a few stairs go to GURUJI's room. When I opened my eyes, I saw a snake going upstairs. I saw GURUJI following him to the stairs.

My eyes remained wide open on the scene I had witnessed. I simply could not believe what I was watching. I almost became numb.

After GURUJI went up, I got up from my place and asked that young boy about it.

He told me, "Aunty, please don't mention what you saw to anyone. This is your personal Darshan!".

I had no words, and it was time to go home now. Before going home, I wanted to use the washroom.

The boy said, "Aunty, as you are going upstairs, so don't stand there. Guruji's room remains open one or two inches. please don't stand there. Just watch and come back".

I followed the young boy's instructions and I can't express what I saw. My surprise was limitless and unbounded

The snake that climbed the stairs was coiled around sitting GURUJI.

The head of the snake was covering GURUJI' s head!

I had shivers in my whole body and goosebumps all across. I ran away from there. I looked at that young boy in surprise. He kept his finger on his lips and asked me not to utter a single word!

I came back home and was in shock for days together on what I saw and felt that day! Even today, when I think about it, I get goosebumps all across.

I couldn't be less grateful for these beautiful BLESSINGS I received from Guruji.

# Guruji Takes Away Your Pains and Sufferings

"Those blessings are sweetest that are won with prayer and worn with thanks."

— *Thomas Goodwin*

There is no pain in the world that Guruji Maharaj cannot take away or free you from its suffering. Guruji can show a new way of life even in the grimmest of the situation and sends a light of hope amidst the biggest chaos of life. In one of such incidents when one of my closest people in life - my Uncle has left the world, I was sailed through that grief only with the blessings of life. I was surprised how he can listen to our heart's things, even when he is not present around. My month's long grief and suffering ended on just reaching his abode. That's the power of divine Guruji Maharaj.

In the Year 2015 we used to live in the Delhi Vasant Kunj area but our other house was in Gurgaon. It was turned into a PG while we were staying in Vasant Kunj. However, we vacated this house in 2015 and shifted to Gurgaon after staying for 25 years in the Vasant Kunj area of Delhi.

It was here that I got connected to Gurgaon Sangat.

One day all of a sudden, my Uncle developed heart pain in the office. He was working at the Airport Authority of India in November 2016. We shifted him immediately to the hospital, but he, unfortunately, could not survive and passed away soon. He was the closest person in my life and I couldn't bear his sudden demise. I stayed indoors, mourning his death for almost one month.

One day my daughter-in-law said —"Why don't you go out for some time for a change? Where do you want to go, Maa?

The coincidence was such that It was a Monday. I got up to be ready for the visit to Bada Mandir. My daughter-in-law told me strictly not to wear shabby clothes or lightly shaded clothes.

Finally, I headed to Bada Mandir with watery eyes crying and a heavy heart all the way to Bada Mandir.

From Chhatarpur Metro Station, the car turned right, and all of a sudden, my eyes caught a glimpse of hoarding on the signal. It was written -OLX. Seeing that board a strange thought came to my mind and I talked to in my head in this way

I instantly said- "Bada Mandir!"

"Guruji Maharaj, things are sold on OLX. I also want to sell something. I want to sell my grief. Will you buy it?"

I was conversing with Guruji Maharaj by questioning and answering myself on his behalf

"Guruji Maharaj what is the price at which you will buy my grief?

Guruji Maharaj said-" Whatever price you will fix, I will double it!"

I kept on talking to myself like this the whole way, settling for the price of my grief to Guruji and in no time, I reached the Bada Mandir.

I went inside the Mandir and did my Darshan. Then I went to Langar hall and ate the Samosa Prasad. After that, I reached my car and started my way back to home.

I couldn't believe that my grief was sold and there was no more tears tsunami in my eyes. My mind and my heart were suddenly at peace.

I never looked back after that and Guruji Maharaj wiped my tears. He made me cheerful with his blessings. Today, I am a happy and very  contented person in life.

This is how a Guru can relieve you of your grief and sufferings. So, talk to him and share your heart's concern with your Guruji. He will show you the path of happiness and contentment in life.

"When you focus on being a blessing, God makes sure that you are always blessed in abundance."

— *Joel Osteen*

# Guruji's Childhood Memories

"I believe that whatever comes at a particular time is a blessing from God".

Guruji was the divine Avatar of Shiva. Those who spent time with him swear by certain events and happening that made everyone believe that he has some supernatural power and was not a normal child. I will narrate some of the very interesting and miraculous events of his childhood in this write- up. We could know about these happenings only when his mother came in and dropped by.

We were sitting in Jalandhar at his Darbar when suddenly everyone around us heard that Guruji Maharaji's mother had come to meet him. It was a delightful moment for all of us to know the mother of such a divine soul.

We all sat around her, surrounding her to know the tales of Guruji's childhood. His mother told us multiple tales that made us believe that he was not a normal child and he never did any normal things that children would usually do in their childhood.

In one incident, she told us that once Guruji Maharaj wanted to play with his friends when he was pretty young, but his friends refused to play because they had exams the next day.

At the constant request of Guruji Maharaj, they agreed to play and stayed back with him. After the play, when they were going back, Guruji Maharaj told them to open their book and study certain topics. He told them that these topics would come in the exam. Children studied them, and to their surprise, all questions were the same!

In another such incident, one day Guruji and his friends were playing the game of marbles. Everyone realized that wherever Guruji Maharaj used to say that the marble would go after the hit, it went there. He knew the things so closely!

Once Guruji was appearing in his final exams in school. One of his friend's pen ink finished.

Guruji Maharaj asked his friend to give him his pen. Guruji Maharaj filled this pen's ink without the inkpot. The teacher invigilating was watching it and noticed it. He also emptied both his pens and told Guruji Maharaj to fill them up with ink. Guruji Maharaj instantly filled the pens-one with blue ink and another with red ink. The teacher was surprised to see that how he fill the pen ink without an ink pot. He was convinced there and then that  he was not a normal child.

In childhood, one of the Gurujis' Tayaji Son was his teacher and one day; he told Guruji Maharaj to learn the spellings of Sunflower and Cauliflower, but he was too young and he couldn't do that. He gave him a tight slap on this incidence  When he realized later on that that he was a Mahapurush, he regretted it profoundly.

One day Guruji Maharaj's friend came to Guruji Maharaj's house and said they wanted to eat halva. They had seen great poverty and Guruji Maharaji's mother said that there is nothing to make halva in the house.

Guruji Maharaj said to his mother that she should burn the fire and place the vessel on the fire. He told her that she must keep stirring the vessel. Listening to his son, she kept stirring the empty vessel. All of a sudden, to everyone's surprise, the vessel was full of halva. It was Sach Khand Prasad.

Once Guru ji's middle brother bought a cow and brought it home. When Guruji Maharaj saw that he got annoyed and asked him to return the cow, he predicted that his brother had brought the kaal for himself. The brother didn't listen to him and said that the cow would give the milk and the whole family will benefit from it. He did not listen to Guruji that day.

A few days later, the same cow hit the brother with her horns in the stomach. All these incidents time and again proved that Guruji was never a normal child and he was a live Shiva incarnation. Nothing is hidden from Guruji.

We were blessed to be living a life with such a divine soul and were really lucky to spend that valuable time of our life with Guruji.


"There's a blessing in everything that happens to us".

# Guruji's Jaani Jaan

"When you are grateful - when you can see what you have - you unlock blessings to flow in your life."

— Suze Orman

I will narrate an incident where I was surprised to know that Guruji Maharaj has an idea about the past, present and future. He is the one who calls us and drives the meetings in an ever-busy world.

As my uncle was in Air Force, he used to go for inspection from time to time with all his commanders. He was a pilot. On one such occasion, I took the opportunity to go to Jalandhar to meet Guruji Maharaj. I was delighted that this time I will have full four days with Guruji.

In those days, there were only landline phones. I took the receiver from the phone and kept it down so that all the time phone shows that it is engaged.

So, I took a bus and went to ISBT and then went to Jalandhar waiting to reach Guruji all my way. I reached in the evening. The next day I was in Guruji's Darbar in Jalandhar by morning 9:00 a.m.

I spent the full three days with Guruji Maharaj, this time 9 a.m. To 9 p.m. Guruji Maharaj blessed everyone with Jal Prasad except me for three days! I was not offered the Jal Prasad even once in these three days. On the fourth day, I went to Guruji Maharaj. I bowed my head to Guruji Maharaji and begged for his permission to leave for Delhi.

Guruji Maharaj denied and asked me to go the next day. I told

Guruji Maharaj that my uncle is about to come, and I would be scolded if I am not there. Guruji Maharaj laughed and said that his airplane had undergone some issues in Bangalore and he will come tomorrow. So, you also go tomorrow.

We never had the audacity to say no to Guruji. I stayed back that day and Guruji Maharaj called me up and said-"So, what did you think that you did not receive the Prasad even once?"

I was surprised to see that Guruji knew exactly what I was thinking! That day Guruji Maharaj made me drink three big glasses of Jal Prasad and did my soul cleansing. My purpose for the trip was fulfilled and I was so grateful.

The fourth day, I took his permission and reached Delhi. To my surprise, my Uncle had not reached yet. After he came, he asked me the reason that why I did not pick up the phone?

I wanted to inform you that I will come the next day as my airplane has some mechanical issues in Bangalore. I was smiling in my heart. I told him that my phone was out of order and no ringtone was Coming.

This incidence reaffirmed to me that Guru Ji knows what all is happening in the world!

Lots of Love and Blessings

"When I started counting my blessings, my whole life turned."

— *Willie Nelson*

# Kamlesh Aunty Ji Satsang

"Count your blessings, not your problems."

Your Guru can protect you in the toughest of times. When you feel scared and nobody is there with you, your Guru is the one who holds your hand even when you can't see him. In one such incident, when Punjab was grappling with terror, and it was not safe travelling in the odd hours, I realized the invisible presence of Guruji Maharaj to protect me and keep me safe.

Once I travelled to Punjab in winters to visit Guruji Maharaj in Jalandhar. I had an overnight stay in Chandigarh and the next day I travelled to Jalandhar. I reached in good two hours from Chandigarh to reach Guruji. I didn't realize that it was 7 p.m; while leaving in the evening and it had become dark enough to be late for me to stay out. Those were the days of terrorism in Punjab.

I looked at Guruji Maharaj in a concerned way as to how to go back now?

He said, "Go with the rickshaw that standing outside."

As I went out and saw that there was a rickshaw standing there. A Sardar Ji owned this rickshaw looked at me and asked me to sit. I sat in the Riksha and left the Darbar.

1 saw that it had really gone late and we could not even see the road number. There were no street lights and it was pitch dark. Only a small little lamplight of his Riksha was showing the way on the road. There was no one on the road as everyone used to go indoors before the dark.

In the silence of this darkness, the Rikshawala started singing the Shabad of Guruji and he was singing it so melodiously that I didn't know how my travel time passed. His Shabad were so mesmerizing. Soon I reached home and I didn't even know it. The travel was so enjoyable.

When the door opened, I saw that everybody was surprised to see me;

How did I travel at that part of the night?

The next day when I went to Guruji Maharaj, he asked me if I enjoyed the Shabad?

I was surprised to know that he knew the last night's happening!

I asked him how he knew that the rickshaw puller was singing the Shabad when you were here. I couldn't believe what he said!

He said that a Guru could be at ten places at one time. I felt so blessed that my Guruji Maharaj was with me in all difficult times. So, be assured that if you have decided to hold the hands of Guruji Maharaj, then he would be present with you always. You just need to remember him and he will be there at your rescue. Have full faith in your Guruji.

"When we lose one blessing, another is often most unexpetedly given in its place."

Lots of Love and Blessings

# Positive Attitude is an Advantage

"Keep your face always toward the sunshine - and shadows will fall behind you."

— *Waft Whitman*

We all talk about a positive attitude, but we hardly know what a positive attitude can bring to our lives. Your positive attitude can change your life and destiny forever. This is my take on this strong attitudinal trait. I learned it from my Guruji Maharaj to be positive in all kinds of situations in life.

A positive attitude is not just about sporting a smile. It is about maintaining an optimistic attitude and mindset. It is about your attitude in the uttermost chaos. Just like a good or bad diet can affect your body, positive and negative thoughts also do the same to your mind. So, feed your mind with positive thoughts, and amazing changes around you.

When you start thinking optimistically, your mind gets clear of any negative thoughts, and you can see the world in a new light. Very soon, you will stop blaming yourself or others. You will be in total control of your emotions. So, it's important to try and seek valuable lessons in every setback and experience

A positive attitude is known to be linked with a feeling of happiness. But what is happiness? Happiness is a state of mind that comes from within, and it is not dependent on external factors. When you think positively, you will be in a state of harmony and happiness. So, with a positive attitude, you can be happy right now, irrespective of any situation you are in.

When you develop a positive attitude, you will start feeling better yourself. You will treat yourself with more respect and love. This, in turn, will boost your confidence levels and inner strength. You will take out new challenges and overcome your limiting beliefs.

With positive thinking, you can achieve a motivational balance. You learn to stay focused, and as a result, you can come up with the right decisions in the most challenging situations. You can train your mind to stay positive in several ways. Repeating positive affirmations is a great way to train your mind to think positively. Reading inspirational and motivational quotes daily will help you overcome the negative thoughts and instill a sense of optimism in you.

Whenever any unpleasant event occurs, try to approach it with a positive mindset and learn an optimistic lesson out of it. Remember your thoughts determine your feelings and actions. So, whenever any negative thought comes to your mind, immediately replace it with a positive one.

"It's not what happens to you, but how you react to it that matters."

— *Epictetus*

# Lassi Prasad

"Blessed are they who see beautiful things in humble places
where other people see nothing."

Whatever Prasad Guru ji gave us was always as Divine as himself, whether it was a Kara Prasad, Langar Prasad, Jal Prasad and Chai Prasad.

What is Prasad?

Prasad is blessed food which is  distributed to everyone and symbolises the belief in equality and the oneness of humanity. Prashad in Gurudwara turned to be blessed once it enters the door of Gurudwara or any sacred place.

500 years ago, Guru Nanak ji started Kada Prasad, which is made with four ingredients- Wheat Flour, Ghee, Sugar and Water. All age groups enjoy the taste of it because it is smooth, soft, velvety and rich in color. Does that mean our Guruji followed the same path which Guru Nanak ji showed to all of us? Langar Prasad is a special Spiritual Prasad, it is blessed by our Divine Guru ji and distributed amongst each one of us. Sevadar and Sangat offer Ardas to Guruji in order to get the Langar Prashad blessed. Sangat in millions being treated mentally, physically and medically with the help of Guruji blessed Langar Prashad.

Guruji was very fond of "LASSI". One of the Sangat (aunty) who was residing in Kishangarh was asked by Guruji to get the Lassi for him every day. This was a Seva, which was offered to her by Guruji. It was her blessings as Guruji was removing her kashat by Lassi.

One day, her children troubled her a lot and it became big chaos in the house. The whole family was fighting with each other. Aunty was so fed up and said in anger: "Mai aa lassi da sayapa karva hai mai dasni hu". She went to Guruji and offered the Lassi to him. Guruji didn't accept the Lassi and threw it away. Earlier, Guru ji used to consume it immediately but that day he refused. Aunty said "Guruji lassi dava".

Guruji replied to her "mai sayapa wali lassi ne peeta mein."

Sangatji, Guru ji could predict what was happening and what is happening in the Universe. He is not limited by time, infact, he is a creator of time. He used to say I know what is happening on this side and the other side of the wall. Guru ji will always guide you to the correct side of your life!

"Live your life for God and God will lead your
life to a world full of Love and True Happiness"

# How Guruji Gave Me a New Life

"One who is guarded by or protected by God, cannot be killed by anyone"

A SMALL GRATITUDE TO MY SATGURU LOTUS FEET

GRATITUDE .... What is gratitude

GRATITUDE .... Thanks

GRATITUDE .... Dhanyawad

GRATITUDE .... Is the echo of Universe.

GRATITUDE .... Is the purest form of self

GRATITUDE .... Is the original voice of God.

GRATITUDE .... When we say thanks to anybody.

GRATITUDE .... When we feel very much in debt to him.

GRATITUDE .... When we feel delightful with him.

GRATITUDE .... When he has done good for us.

GRATITUDE .... When he has fulfilled every desire

GRATITUDE .... We say thanks when our any desire gets gratification

GRATITUDE .... When we get help from anybody

GRATITUDE .... The truth of nature when no man can give Dhanyawad to other. Its our GURU Himself who is thanking.

GRATITUDE .... When all our CHAKRAS get aligned and the energy flows with the feeling of thanks

GRATITUDE .... When the flow of gratitude opens .... one need not to say it

GRATITUDE .... Gratitude thanks comes from inside.

GRATITUDE .... So thanks dhanyawad is checking. KIRPA

GRATITUDE .... We internally feel that, for little little things.

GRATITUDE .... Gratitude is coming from inside that means GURUJI is thanking us. He is happy with our progress.

GRATITUDE .... We are tuned to his blessings.

GRATITUDE .... His blessings will automatically travel towards us.

I celebrated my birthday with Guruji and on the same day, all of a sudden, I had developed a chest pain. I thought it was gas but that persisted the whole day. Next day it became unbearable, so I landed up in the Hospital. Guruji's sangat is not less than a family and I was blessed to be a part of it.

Before I reached the hospital, they were there. Doctor reported that coronary artery was blocked. A cardiac stunt was used to treat my blocked coronary arteries. I came back home on 4th day of the hospitalization.

In between my BP shoot up and I had fallen in washroom twice. With that fall, the stunt had came off and internal bleeding had started. There was no reason for this.

My blood report was not in my favour and again I had to fight with the pain My vision had left my side and I wasn't able to see anything. Then again GURUJI'S sangat came to my rescue. I was taken to the hospital at 11:30 p.m. GURUJI sangat is the most blessed sangat, one could ever find. I thank Aman uncle for always being a messenger of GURUJI. He was there, holding the stretcher at the emergency gate. I had admitted and moved to operation theatre with GURUJI's grace. The stunt had to replace with ballooning process as my many arteries were blocked. I was shifted to ICU at 3 a.m. Mentally and physically tired, I could only Simran GURUJI GURUJI and nothing else.

Jai GURU Ji

When I gained my consciousness, I started talking to GURUJI. "GURUJI, I am in the same hospital (ARTEMIS Hospital) where Ravnik Singh, the owner of this hospital, who was on the wheelchair for several years, was treated. You held his hand and made him stand by his own. With your blessing, he was able to eat the whole burger, which wasn't possible earlier. Here, I request you Guru ji to please hold my hand as well and take me out of this agony and self-pity situation".

While I was talking to him and somewhere, I felt that GURUJI fed me some kind of Chinese burger. I was eating what he was feeding to me. Thanks for those blessings GURUJI. I had given a new life by Guruji.

Next day morning, I noticed all sorts of tubes around my legs, the staff was trying hard to find my veins. And Tracheostomy was performed to save my life. I had to lie down in the straight position only. I wasn't able to turn around for days. But I was hopeful" GURUJI HAY NA" I only recited GURUJI, GURUJI and only GURUJI.

My belief in Guruji didn't let me down and I survived the situation gracefully. Guruji came in my dream in the ICU, he showered his blessing on all the patients in the ward including the ward boy, nurses and other staff, who were looking after me, and he blessed me too.

Sangat ji, the faith in your GURU helps you to conquer the world.

I had heard "Bhaha Farday Na" - he holds your hands to take you out of the difficult situations. Yes, he can turn around the impossible things into possible ones. Now I am blessed to witness the same, Yes the Divine the Lotus Feet always stands by you in any situation. Just call him and you will feel a tap at your shoulder.

Just rekindle your love, faith and Simran towards Guruji

ALL YOUR PRAYERS ARE ANSWERED.

ADORE THE ALMIGHTY and HE WILL ADORE YOU.
IT IS RECRODAL

"What goes around comes around. Do good and good will
follow you"